FRANCIS FRITH'S

EXMOUTH

PHOTOGRAPHIC MEMORIES

JOHN BAINBRIDGE was born in Staffordshire but now lives in Devon, where he works as a freelance writer and researcher. He has spent much of his life exploring our countryside on foot, and has written and broadcast widely about the topography, history and environment of the British Isles.

FRANCIS FRITH'S
PHOTOGRAPHIC MEMORIES

EXMOUTH

PHOTOGRAPHIC MEMORIES

JOHN BAINBRIDGE

First published in the United Kingdom in 2006 by
The Francis Frith Collection®

Hardback Edition 2006 ISBN 1-84589-067-1

Paperback Edition 2006 ISBN 1-84589-035-3

British Library Cataloguing in Publication Data

Exmouth - Photographic Memories
John Bainbridge

The Francis Frith Collection
Frith's Barn, Teffont,
Salisbury, Wiltshire SP3 5QP
Tel: +44 (0) 1722 716 376
Email: info@francisfrith.co.uk
www.francisfrith.co.uk

Printed and bound in Great Britain

Front Cover: **EXMOUTH**, *The Esplanade 1906* 53941t
Frontispiece: **EXMOUTH**, *The Sands 1906* 53938

The colour-tinting is for illustrative purposes only, and is not intended to be historically accurate

Aerial photographs reproduced under licence from Simmons Aerofilms Limited.
Historical Ordnance Survey maps reproduced under licence from Homecheck.co.uk
Every attempt has been made to contact copyright holders of illustrative material. We will be happy to give full acknowledgement in future editions for any items not credited. Any information should be directed to The Francis Frith Collection.

AS WITH ANY HISTORICAL DATABASE THE FRITH ARCHIVE IS CONSTANTLY BEING CORRECTED AND IMPROVED AND THE PUBLISHERS WOULD WELCOME INFORMATION ON OMISSIONS OR INACCURACIES

CONTENTS

FRANCIS FRITH
VICTORIAN PIONEER

FRANCIS FRITH, founder of the world-famous photographic archive, was a complex and multi-talented man. A devout Quaker and a highly successful Victorian businessman, he was philosophical by nature and pioneering in outlook.

By 1855 he had already established a wholesale grocery business in Liverpool, and sold it for the astonishing sum of £200,000, which is the equivalent today of over £15,000,000. Now a very rich man, he was able to indulge his passion for travel. As a child he had pored over travel books written by early explorers, and his fancy and imagination had been stirred by family holidays to the sublime mountain regions of Wales and Scotland. 'What lands of spirit-stirring and enriching scenes and places!' he had written. He was to return to these scenes of grandeur in later years to 'recapture the thousands of vivid and tender memories', but with a different purpose. Now in his thirties, and captivated by the new science of photography, Frith set out on a series of pioneering journeys up the Nile and to the Near East that occupied him from 1856 until 1860.

INTRIGUE AND EXPLORATION

These far-flung journeys were packed with intrigue and adventure. In his life story, written when he was sixty-three, Frith tells of being held captive by bandits, and of fighting 'an awful midnight battle to the very point of surrender with a deadly pack of hungry, wild dogs'. Wearing flowing Arab costume, Frith arrived at Akaba by camel sixty years before Lawrence of Arabia, where he encountered 'desert princes and rival sheikhs, blazing with jewel-hilted swords'.

He was the first photographer to venture beyond the sixth cataract of the Nile. Africa was still the mysterious 'Dark Continent', and Stanley and Livingstone's historic meeting was a decade into the future. The conditions for picture taking confound belief. He laboured for hours in his wicker dark-room in the sweltering heat of the desert, while the volatile chemicals fizzed dangerously in their trays. Back in London he exhibited his photographs and was 'rapturously cheered' by members of the Royal Society. His reputation as a photographer was made overnight.

VENTURE OF A LIFE-TIME

Characteristically, Frith quickly spotted the opportunity to create a new business as a specialist publisher of photographs. He lived in an era of immense and sometimes violent

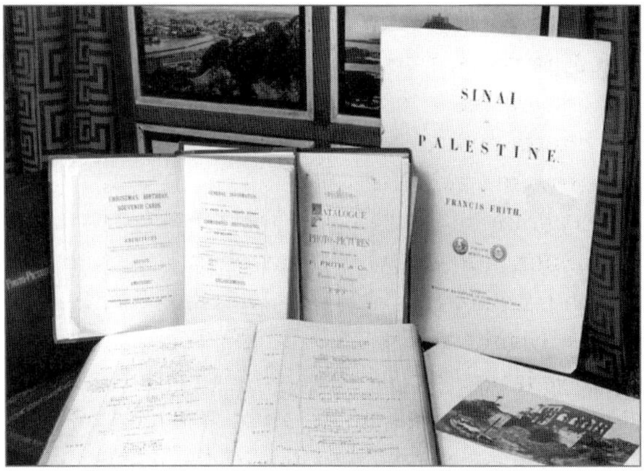

change. For the poor in the early part of Victoria's reign work was exhausting and the hours long, and people had precious little free time to enjoy themselves. Most had no transport other than a cart or gig at their disposal, and rarely travelled far beyond the boundaries of their own town or village. However, by the 1870s the railways had threaded their way across the country, and Bank Holidays and half-day Saturdays had been made obligatory by Act of Parliament. All of a sudden the working man and his family were able to enjoy days out and see a little more of the world.

With typical business acumen, Francis Frith foresaw that these new tourists would enjoy having souvenirs to commemorate their days out. In 1860 he married Mary Ann Rosling and set out on a new career: his aim was to photograph every city, town and village in Britain. For the next thirty years he travelled the country by train and by pony and trap, producing fine photographs of seaside resorts and beauty spots that were keenly bought by millions of Victorians. These prints were painstakingly pasted into family albums and pored over during the dark nights of winter, rekindling precious memories of summer excursions.

THE RISE OF FRITH & CO

Frith's studio was soon supplying retail shops all over the country. To meet the demand he gathered about him a small team of photographers, and published the work of independent artist-photographers of the calibre of Roger Fenton and Francis Bedford. In order to gain some understanding of the scale of Frith's business one only has to look at the catalogue issued by Frith & Co in 1886: it runs to some 670 pages, listing not only many thousands of views of the British Isles but also many photographs of most European countries, and China, Japan, the USA and Canada - note the sample page shown on page 9 from the hand-written Frith & Co ledgers recording the pictures. By 1890 Frith had created the greatest specialist photographic publishing company in the world, with over 2,000 sales outlets - more than the combined number that Boots and WH Smith have today! The picture on the next page shows the Frith & Co display board at Ingleton in the Yorkshire Dales (left of window). Beautifully constructed with a mahogany frame and gilt inserts, it could display up to a dozen local scenes.

POSTCARD BONANZA

The ever-popular holiday postcard we know today took many years to develop. In 1870 the Post Office issued the first plain cards, with a pre-printed stamp on one face. In 1894 they allowed other publishers' cards to be sent through the mail with an attached adhesive halfpenny stamp. Demand grew rapidly, and in 1895 a new size of postcard was permitted called the court card, but there was little room for illustration. In 1899, a year after Frith's death, a new card measuring 5.5 x 3.5 inches became the standard format, but it was not until 1902 that the divided back came into being, so that the address and message could be on one face and a full-size illustration on the other. Frith & Co were in the vanguard of postcard development: Frith's sons Eustace and Cyril continued their father's monumental task, expanding the number of views offered to the public and recording more and more places

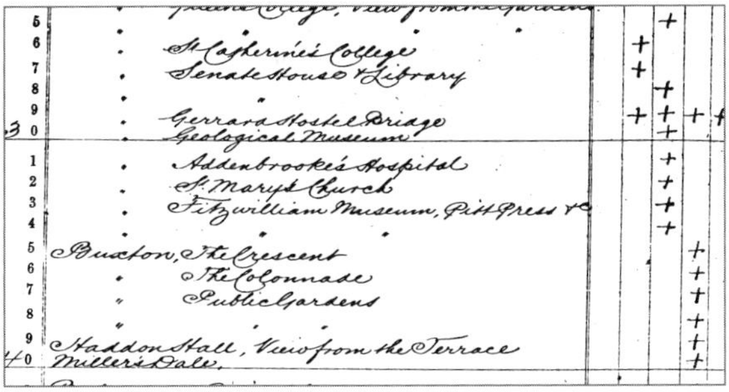

in Britain, as the coasts and countryside were opened up to mass travel.

Francis Frith had died in 1898 at his villa in Cannes, his great project still growing. The archive he created continued in business for another seventy years. By 1970 it contained over a third of a million pictures showing 7,000 British towns and villages.

FRANCIS FRITH'S LEGACY

Frith's legacy to us today is of immense significance and value, for the magnificent archive of evocative photographs he created provides a unique record of change in the cities, towns and villages throughout Britain over a century and more. Frith and his fellow studio photographers revisited locations many times down the years to update their views, compiling for us an enthralling and colourful pageant of British life and character.

We are fortunate that Frith was dedicated to recording the minutiae of everyday life, for it is this sheer wealth of visual data, the painstaking chronicle of changes in dress, transport, street layouts, buildings, housing, engineering and landscape that captivates us so much today. His remarkable images offer us a powerful link with the past and with the lives of our ancestors.

THE VALUE OF THE ARCHIVE TODAY

Computers have now made it possible for Frith's many thousands of images to be accessed almost instantly. Frith's images are increasingly used as visual resources, by social historians, by researchers into genealogy and ancestry, by architects and town planners, and by teachers involved in local history projects.

In addition, the archive offers every one of us an opportunity to examine the places where we and our families have lived and worked down the years. Highly successful in Frith's own era, the archive is now, a century and more on, entering a new phase of popularity. Historians consider the Francis Frith Collection to be of prime national importance. It is the only archive of its kind remaining in private ownership. Francis Frith's archive is now housed in an historic timber barn in the beautiful village of Teffont in Wiltshire. Its founder would not recognize the archive office as it is today. In place of the many thousands of dusty boxes containing glass plate negatives and an all-pervading odour of photographic chemicals, there are now ranks of computer screens. He would be amazed to watch his images travelling round the world at unimaginable speeds through internet lines.

The archive's future is both bright and exciting. Francis Frith, with his unshakeable belief in making photographs available to the greatest number of people, would undoubtedly approve of what is being done today with his lifetime's work. His photographs depicting our shared past are now bringing pleasure and enlightenment to millions around the world a century and more after his death.

EXMOUTH
AN INTRODUCTION

EXMOUTH is proud of the fact that it is the oldest seaside resort in Devon, a town that attracted fashionable Georgian society in great numbers and now draws in an equally delighted but much wider range of society.

Yet while the resort is old, the town is new. Long ago the parishes of Littleham and Withycombe Raleigh were the main settlements in the area, villages whose heartlands were further away from the sea than Exmouth is today. Exmouth, if anything, was a kind of tiny fishing suburb, though it has long absorbed these ancient parishes.

The resort owes much to its setting, located as it is on a spit of land between the waters of Lyme Bay and the mighty estuary of the River Exe, all sand and mud banks here as it widens and then suddenly narrows to meet the tide in a tiny channel between Exmouth Point and the beaches of Dawlish Warren - a place that feels more sea than land.

To the east and north there is higher ground, the cliffs of Orcombe and the great ridges of heathland that radiate from the Iron Age Woodbury Castle. It was from here that the first settlers probably descended to the lower ground, seeking better agricultural land, fish to eat, and salt from the sea to preserve food.

The *Anglo-Saxon Chronicle* tells us that in the year 1001 the Danes, led by Sweyn their king, sailed into the Exe, probably destroying the modest hamlets around what is now Exmouth, before attacking Exeter. It is one of the district's earliest mentions in history. In the years that followed, Exmouth developed as a port of such importance that by 1346 it could provide ten ships and 1,100 seaman to support King Edward III's attack on Calais.

Exmouth's martial story does not end there. During the English Civil War a fort was held for King Charles I on the slight rise of ground that is now Gun Cliff Gardens; for all its modest size, it held out against superior Parliamentary forces for several weeks in 1646.

For much of the next two centuries, Exmouth remained vulnerable to attack from Dutch and French naval vessels and privateers. On a memorable day in 1782 Exmouthians and 'society' visitors watched the Dutch privateer 'Zeuse' defeated by the British naval vessel 'Defiance' just offshore. The sole British casualty, an Exmouth seaman called William Bence, was interred with great honour in Littleham churchyard.

This was no doubt a spectacular occasion for the tourists who were already flocking to the resort. Exmouth's history as a watering place began around 1720 when the wealthier members of early Georgian society found their way to the town, lured by tales of its warm climate and pleasant surroundings. Just ten years after the battle with the 'Zeuse', the first six houses were erected on the high ground of the Beacon, all with excellent views across the Channel and the Exe estuary.

Much of the land belonged to the Rolle family, whose succeeding generations saw the benefits of developing the resort for health and seaside bathing. The historian Polwhele, a fair propagandist for the delights of so much of Devon, told his readers: 'It (Exmouth) is well sheltered from the north-east and south-west winds by some high hills which rise almost close behind it, and which will supply the place with excellent water'.

The Napoleonic Wars, which closed the Continent to the wealthier traveller, brought new visitors and prosperity to the town; as much might be said for the much-paraded benefits of sea bathing, promoted at not so distant Weymouth by King George III. Exmouth's long sands, gently sloping into the sea, and safe once away from the river mouth and the weedy stretch offshore from the Maer, could have been made for this relatively new activity.

Exmouth's sea front at this time was very different to how we see it today. The long sea wall and esplanade did not exist; between the growing town and the sands was a landscape of marshland and dunes, with animals grazing on the meadows overlooking the sea. The waters of the estuary came well into what is now the heart of the town. The Strand was literally a strand, its houses and early shops occasionally washed by the high tide. A tale is told of residents manoeuvring around the area in washing tubs to avoid getting their feet - and much else - wet.

Exmouth was never as fashionable as the more popular Georgian resorts and health spas, such as Brighton or Weymouth or Bath. There was less to do, and the Assembly Rooms on the Beacon (now a restaurant) were modest in comparison to those in the premier resorts. Visitors came to bathe, to walk, to seek the fresh air, to relax, or to escape from the over-burdening pressures of a gossiping and busy society.

THE SANDS *1922* 72956

Some sought exile in Exmouth to get away from scandal. The first such social refugee was Mary Anne Clarke, ex-mistress of the Duke of York, the improvident second son of King George III. The Duke spent a fortune on keeping Mary Anne in a style to which she rapidly became accustomed. But this was not enough, and she soon found a way to make even more money. The Duke was commander-in-chief of the army, and Mary Anne added to her income by selling military appointments to dozens of Georgian gentlemen. When the ensuing scandal threatened to consume the royal family, Mary Anne was pensioned off to live quietly in distant Exmouth.

She took a property, Chester House, which may still be seen in Imperial Road, and lived in great style. When the money she had been promised by the near bankrupt duke failed to arrive, she blackmailed him, threatening to publish their risqué correspondence. Her plot worked, and she was paid a fortune to keep quiet. After further litigation she removed from Exmouth to serve a period in prison before exiling herself to Boulogne, where she died some years later.

On the other side of town, at Number 6 The Beacon, lived Lady Nelson, wife of the naval admiral and hero of Trafalgar. Lord and Lady Nelson separated in 1801, following his deeper love for Lady Hamilton. Lady Nelson came to live in Exmouth in 1816, becoming a popular member of local society, famed for her parties and balls. She died in 1831 and is buried in Littleham churchyard in the same tomb as the son of her first marriage, Captain Josiah Nesbit, and several of her grandchildren.

Nearby at Number 19 The Beacon lived Lady Byron, estranged wife of the Romantic poet. She had separated from Byron after just a year of marriage, and came to live in Exmouth in 1823. It is said that Lady Byron was a tearful and reclusive figure during her stay in the town, much given to staring out

THE ESPLANADE *1906* 53941

to sea and taking solitary walks. The Beacon attracted other well known society figures in the century that followed, including the King of Saxony, who gave the word 'Royal' to the Royal Beacon Hotel, where he stayed for a brief visit in 1844.

Perhaps the strangest residents of the area were the Misses Parminter, two eccentric maiden ladies who built the strange sixteen-sided circular house A La Ronde just outside the town in 1798. The unusual house's rooms surround an octagonal central hall, topped by a gallery covered in sea shells. Nearby they built a chapel, Point-in-View, so that they would not have to make the journey into Exmouth for their Sunday worship. These reclusive ladies found their last rest here, within yards of the peculiar home they created.

Exmouth came into its own as a seaside resort during Queen Victoria's reign, particularly after the opening of the railway in 1861 made access to the area much easier than it had been in the days of the stagecoach. But Exmouth remained a town of modest size compared to the sprawling resort it is today. Smuggling flourished as a considerable local industry well into the 19th century, mostly under the control of the famous Jack Rattenbury and the Mutter family, though the increase in a watchful population and the building of the sea wall inhibited the landing of contraband in the immediate vicinity of the town.

The way the town developed was probably most influenced by the building of the sea wall in 1842; this was a massive feat of engineering, given the sheer length of Exmouth's sea front. Its creation, topped by the Esplanade - a glorious place for a promenade - presented the opportunity to develop the frontage of the town, along with gardens and leisure facilities. Comparing the earliest photographs in this collection with the present scene it is remarkable how little has changed: the more noticeable differences are in the dress of those enjoying their holiday rather than the background. The Victorians and Edwardians that we see here were the creators of the traditional seaside holiday that endured well into the 20th century – a stay by the sea was now more about sheer enjoyment than health issues.

Exmouth escaped the worst ravages of the Second World War, though some areas such as Chapel Hill were heavily bombed. The sea front was protected from enemy landings by a great sheath of barbed wire, and the docks were protected by anti-aircraft guns. Allied troops were stationed in and around the town, and there were military camps on the outskirts.

In the decades that followed, Exmouth regained its position as a premier resort, though it always catered for those seeking a quieter holiday, emphasising the glory of the sandy beaches and the natural beauty of Exmouth's setting. There were the gardens lining the long Esplanade in which to sit, the cliffs and heathlands for country rambles, and entertainments such as the Pavilion Theatre with its impressive programme of plays, concerts and shows. For the younger generation there were donkey rides, a miniature railway, and a boating pond. Some families would come year after year for the traditional fortnight in August, and for several decades a multitude of hotels and guest houses thrived.

The very nature of this sort of seaside holiday changed in the last years of the 20th century owing to the growth of cheap foreign holidays and an industrial recession. People do still come to Exmouth for longer holidays, but the town does not really have the old August high season any more, with the consequent sad loss of some of the older hotels. There is now a greater emphasis on short breaks, weekend visits, and day trips. Visitors to Exmouth are more likely to stay in bed and breakfast establishments than hotels. Harking back to the Georgian visitors' practice, today's holidaymakers more commonly rent an apartment, or perhaps a caravan at one of the neighbouring camping sites. Coaches bring day trippers from towns and cities across the West Country and other parts of England.

Many have chosen to make Exmouth their home, and the population has increased dramatically in the last fifty years; suburbs now sprawl out into the original parishes of Withycombe Raleigh and Littleham, though both of these have somehow managed to preserve their village hearts.

The closure of the docks at the end of the last century has led to a massive redevelopment of the dock area, with luxury apartments standing where ships once unloaded and men worked long hours. But boats still set out on fishing expeditions, and the old ferry bumbles across the Exe estuary to Starcross. The estuary itself has now been recognised as a bird sanctuary of international importance, attracting bird-watchers from around the world.

The heart of Exmouth is little changed since these photographs were taken. It is still possible to promenade along the Esplanade as the Victorians and Edwardians we see here did, and to seek the shade of the trees in Madeira Walk, to explore the dunes of the Maer, or search out bargains in the shops of the Strand and Rolle Street. Exmouth is Devon's oldest resort, and still displays its heritage with pride.

THE HARBOUR VIEW CAFÉ *c1955* E52018

TOWN AND DOCKS

THE HEART of the town has changed little since these photographs were taken, even though Exmouth is now the largest town in the east of Devon. The substantial growth during the last century and the beginning of this present one has taken place in the suburbs.

Exmouth's town centre is fortunate in that it is not dominated by chain stores with the identical shop frontages that make their premises so familiar in any town anywhere. Such stores are mostly confined to one modern shopping centre built in an area devastated by wartime bombing, leaving the original streets alone. These streets have not changed that much, though some familiar shops seen in these photographs and remembered by older Exmouthians are no more. The roads are now much busier with a massive increase in traffic.

The district around the docks has changed very much: the area is now given over to leisure yachting in place of the commercial shipping that dominated the harbour and docks until very recently. It is sad fact that many of the original dockland buildings have been lost, to be replaced with luxury apartments; these photographs are therefore a valuable record of past times.

A GENERAL VIEW *1890* 26256

Exmouth is the oldest of Devon's seaside resorts – it was a watering place for the wealthy from at least the 1720s. It came into its own during the Georgian period, when a number of well-known figures such as Lady Byron and Lady Nelson chose to reside in the town.

THE CLOCK TOWER *1898* 42467

The clock tower on Exmouth's sea front is a good place to begin any exploration of the resort. The foundation stone was laid on 15 September 1897 by Lady Gertrude Rolle in celebration of Queen Victoria's Diamond Jubilee; the site was donated by the Hon Mark Rolle. Today it is the centrepiece of the town's Flagpole Memorial, opened in 1995 to commemorate the 50th anniversary of the end of the Second World War. This newer memorial bears the flags of many nations and a call that all should live in peace.

THE VIKING BOAT *c1955* E52029

This re-enactment of the Viking invasion of Exmouth commemorates one of the earliest events in Exmouth's history. In 1001 the Danish king Sweyn landed with a considerable force, burning and sacking Exmouth before defeating the Saxon army at nearby Pinhoe. There have been several re-enactments in recent years.

THE STRAND GARDENS *1938* 88620

The waters of the Exe estuary once lapped the edge of what is now a pleasant town centre park. In earlier days this was the commercial heart of Exmouth, for it was the setting for fairs in the spring and autumn. The Globe Hotel, the original terminus for stagecoaches from Exeter, was sited here, but it has long since been demolished.

WE WILL REMEMBER THEM

THE STRAND GARDENS *c1955* E52035

The Strand Gardens were laid out in 1870. To the left of the war memorial is Boots the Chemist, with its old-fashioned shop frontage. It is no longer on this site.

THE STRAND GARDENS *c1960* E52053

The Strand has recently recaptured something of its old atmosphere of stalls and booths, for it is now the location for present-day farmers' markets. It remains a restful place for shoppers to sit on the benches around Exmouth's war memorial with its evocative inscription: 'Is It Nothing To All Ye That Pass By'.

THE STRAND *1906* 56767

This earlier view of the Strand shows the Wiltshire & Dorset Bank on the left and the Commercial and Temperance Hotel in the far distance. Just past the bank is Tommy Bickford's chemist's shop. Tommy Bickford was a larger-than-life Exmouth character - he died the year after this photograph was taken.

ROLLE STREET *1895* 36055

Looking back along Rolle Street towards the Strand, we can see how quiet the streets of Exmouth could be towards the end of Queen Victoria's reign. On the left, at the junction with Chapel Street, is Tozer's Stores. John Tozer was famous for his advertising stunts, such as promoting china tea with a native of China. Just beyond is the Co-operative Fancy and Domestic Warehouse. A delivery boy, on the edge of the pavement with a large milk can at his feet, is standing beside a hand cart belonging to Messrs Jefferies of Rolle Street.

▲ **ROLLE STREET** *1906* 53944

Rolle Street takes its name from the Rolle family of Bicton House, who owned the land on which much of modern day Exmouth stands. This broad thoroughfare, seen here where it leaves the Strand, was constructed in 1875. The woman and young girl on the left are standing in the doorway of the local piano shop.

► *detail from* 53944

► THE ROYAL BEACON HOTEL
1906 56771

Exmouth is Devon's oldest seaside resort, and this was reflected in the construction of several early and very prominent hotels. The Royal Beacon Hotel was built c1810 at the end of the fashionable Beacon Terrace. It began its existence as the Marine Hotel, no doubt because of its fine views over the sea and estuary, but became the Beacon Hotel soon afterwards. It acquired the 'Royal' appendage to its name after a visit in 1844 by the King of Saxony.

◄ BEACON TERRACE
1906 56770

In olden days a beacon fire was lit on the headland to alert the countryside to threats of raids and possible invasion. The terrace, begun in 1791, became the place to live for those wealthier members of Georgian society who had settled in Exmouth, including Lady Nelson, the estranged wife of the hero of Trafalgar, and Lady Byron, the abandoned spouse of the famous poet.

▲ **THE PLANTATION** *1890* 26269
▼ **MADEIRA WALK AND THE BOWLING GREEN** *1931* 84076

The Plantation and Madeira Walk below The Beacon and Louisa Terrace are a delightful stretch of green wooded shelter on hot days. These grounds were opened in 1838; they were strictly closed at sunset by a caretaker who would blow a warning horn before fastening the gates - a practice that continued until the start of the 20th century.

MORTON CRESCENT
1895 36053

A young man in a boater smiles at the Frith photographer just in front of the long and impressive Morton Crescent, so little changed since this photograph was taken towards the end of Queen Victoria's long reign.

MORTON CRESCENT *1906* 56769

This Victorian crescent lines one end of Exmouth's long Esplanade. It was built in 1870 for the benefit of the hotel trade in Victoria's reign, and several hotels survive to this day, though some of the buildings are now blocks of flats. Before the buildings runs what is now the very busy road along the sea front. The ornate lamppost is no more, alas!

ALEXANDRA TERRACE *1906* 56768

Alexandra Terrace overlooks the line of Exmouth's sea front, its view as uninterrupted today as when this photograph was taken a century ago. The terrace is relatively unchanged, though there has been the intrusion of modern windows in some of the top storeys. Many of the original houses are now blocks of flats.

THE IMPERIAL HOTEL *c1960* E52111

A damaging fire in 1974 has altered the appearance of the Imperial Hotel since this photograph was taken. The hotel was built in 1868 to capitalise on the huge number of tourists coming to Exmouth during the resort's Victorian heyday. In the grounds were built two imitation Greek temples, one of which - the Temple of Theseus - still survives.

THE CRICKET AND SPORTS GROUND *1906* 53961b

A crowd has gathered and awaits the start of a match at Exmouth's cricket ground, a few hundred yards from the sea front. Change the dress of the spectators, and little has changed from this viewpoint in the past century.

THE PIER *1896* 37624

Exmouth never had a pier in the traditional English seaside sense, just a landing stage to facilitate access to the larger passenger boats that visited the resort. Ships such as the one we see here carried on the passenger trade between the coastal resorts, and steam packets operated between Exmouth and London as early as the 1830s. The advertising hoarding on the pier promoted H Webber, a butcher.

▲ **BEACH BUNGALOWS**
1906 56772

◄ **BEACH BUNGALOWS**
1906 56773

In earlier days a beach community existed: numerous bungalows were built on the sands of the Exe estuary, particularly on the long spit of land known as Dawlish Warren, which stretches to this day across towards - but not quite as far as - Exmouth. Over the years since this photograph was taken, the sea has encroached, and the last of the Warren bungalows vanished in 1946.

THE COASTGUARD STATION *1906* 53959

Two sailors stand just along from the coastguard station in Edwardian Exmouth. Smuggling was rife on the East Devon coast as an organised industry well into the 19th century, hence the strong coastguard presence in every town. By the time this photograph was taken, the coastguards were taking a greater interest in protecting mariners from the power of the sea than seizing contraband.

▲ **THE PIER AND A STEAMER**
1922 72957

A steamer sets out from Exmouth Pier, watched by boatmen on the nearby beach. A poster advertising the Bric a Bracs, an entertainment troupe, adorns the building at the landward end of the pier. Apart from leisure traffic, Exmouth's dockland area was used for the landing and despatch of cargoes, particularly after 1865 when Exmouth became a port in its own right.

► *detail from* 72957

▲ **THE PIER** *1925* 76815

This time, a poster advertises a concert party given by the Mahatmas. This scene has changed a great deal over the past few years with the new Exmouth dockland development. Apartment blocks have now replaced the modest structures that once surrounded the pier. Before the Second World War, in a world free from 'health and safety' restrictions, children learned to swim in the very busy entrance to the port.

◄ *detail from* 76815

THE STARCROSS FERRY *1925* 76819

In 1887 a Mr Brutton inaugurated the first steam ferry across the Exe estuary to Starcross, replacing a more modest traffic of tiny fishing boats that made the same journey. The ferry service is much used today, not least by walkers making their way around the South West Coast Path.

THE HARBOUR *1925* 76818

These residential bungalows lining the harbour have been mostly swept away by hostile tides and the developments of the past century. The whole harbour and dockland area has been the subject of a major housing development over the past few years, leaving photographs such as this one as the only evidence of what was there before.

A COCKLE WOMAN *1906* 53961

This delightful study of a cockle woman on the sands of the Exe estuary shows the importance of the shellfish industry to the area. There are fewer such gatherers these days, and the estuary is better known for bird watching than cockling.

THE HARBOUR ENTRANCE
c1960 E52033

The channel into Exmouth's harbour remains unchanged, but the rest of this scene is now almost unrecognisable. The docks and cranes in the distance have been swept away, to be replaced by luxury apartment blocks and new shops. The bungalows to the left were demolished quite recently, and the site awaits redevelopment as this book was being written.

EXMOUTH *from the air 1953* AFA51154

THE BEACH FROM MORTON CRESCENT *c1898* 37620

In this, the first of five views of the Esplanade taken through time, and seen from the end of Morton Crescent, we notice the clock tower soon after it was built. The carriages gathered around the lamppost were used to convey Victorian tourists along the long sea front. A number of bathing machines are drawn up along the edge of the sea.

THE SEA FRONT

A SEASIDE holiday has always been about much more than a day on the beach. A holiday resort such as Exmouth needs a considerable infrastructure of leisure activities for holidaymakers to enjoy, both as a supplement to activities on the sands and in case of wet weather.

In this selection we see terraces of hotels built with the holidaymaker in mind, such as Morton Crescent, the Pavilion Theatre, which has offered entertainment to visitors for well over sixty years, and the cafés and formal gardens where people can sit or linger on warm days. Here are the boating lake, the miniature railway, and the much-missed sea front swimming pool.

These are places for enjoyment, refuges from the busy town or the heat of the beach on fine summer days. Exmouth's beautifully laid out gardens are always much appreciated by visitors to the town, offering colour in every season. These photographs show that Exmouth has had skilled and imaginative civic gardeners over a very long period of time.

The construction of the long sea wall in 1842 allowed the opening of the present Esplanade, one of the longest stretches of formal sea frontage for promenading in Devon; a walk from the docks takes the promenader to the wilder scenery of the Maer sand dunes and the cliffs of Orcombe. The Esplanade is as popular today as it ever was, both as a facility for a gentle walk or an early morning jog. It offers some of the best maritime views in southern England.

▲ **THE ESPLANADE**
1922 72952
► **THE ESPLANADE**
1925 78595

Motor vehicles have mostly replaced horse-drawn carriages by the first decade after the Great War. Even so, it is possible to linger in the middle of the road - not a pastime to be indulged in on summer days in the 21st century. The bathing machines have mostly disappeared, to be replaced by beach huts and changing tents. By the time of the 1925 photograph, an early telephone box has appeared on the traffic island.

▲ **THE ESPLANADE** *1898* 42458

This view was taken from the building at the very end of Morton Crescent. To the immediate left is the Imperial Hotel, seen in its original architectural design, changed now after the fire in the 1970s.

◄ **THE ESPLANADE** *c1955* E52002

By the middle of the 20th century we see something resembling the modern scene. There is the more familiar red telephone box on the traffic island, a modern post box, and Belisha beacons to aid pedestrians wishing to cross the road. In the centre of the photograph is the white tower of the Pavilion Theatre. Much of the street furniture was removed by the start of the 21st century, leaving a more traffic-dominated Esplanade.

▶ **FROM THE BEACON** *1922*
72950

This fine view looks across the clock tower and Morton Crescent to the estuary of the River Exe, with Starcross and the Haldon Hills in the distance.

▼ **FROM THE PIER**
1906 56775

The construction of a substantial sea wall, seen here in section to the right, led to Exmouth's prosperity as a seaside resort. Before the wall was built, much of the sea front was marshland and sand dunes, and subjected to constant flooding. The first section of the wall was completed in 1842, paid for by the local landowner John Rolle. It was 1,900 feet long and constructed from Devon limestone. The designer was John Smeaton, a veteran engineer and the designer of London Bridge.

THE ESPLANADE ***c1955*** E52028

The wall was designed to deflect the waves that so often come up the English Channel from the south-west on stormy days. This scene has changed little in fifty years, though now a shelter from the wind stands on the position of the nearest bench in the photograph. It was donated by local resident William Frederick Stokes in 1964.

THE ESPLANADE AND THE PIER ***c1955*** E52026

During the Second World War Exmouth had been subjected to a number of air raids and faced the possibility of invasion. The sea wall and beach languished behind a number of barbed wire fences and obstructions, and were guarded by machine gun positions to deter beach landings and anti-aircraft stations to protect the docks, harbour and shipping in the Exe estuary.

THE ESPLANADE *c1955* E52008

Before the building of Morton Crescent, seen here on the right, a house stood here which was nicknamed 'Corpse Castle': Lady Nelson transported the bodies of her son Josiah Nesbit and his children from their original graves in France for reburial in Littleham, and the corpses rested in a house here on the night before the funeral.

THE ESPLANADE
1906 53941

It is a peaceful day in Edwardian Exmouth. The view looks towards Morton Crescent and Alexandra Terrace. A century earlier this part of Exmouth was just a strand, backed by dunes, marsh and pasture. The building of the sea wall and the Esplanade beyond gave a new opportunity for promenading.

ICES
CHOCOLATE

THE ESPLANADE
1922 72955

This is a similar view to 53941 (previous page), taken a little further in to the 20th century; however, not a great deal has changed apart from the fashions. An ice cream and chocolate seller is surrounded by customers on the beach.

THE BOWLING GREEN *1918* 68712x

This is one of Exmouth's two bowling greens - the other is at the back of the town at Phear Park. The high ground beyond is Gun Cliff Gardens, off Carlton Hill. This was the location of a fort during the English Civil War; its guns controlled the sea and estuary approaches to the besieged city of Exeter.

THE ESPLANADE *1925* 76813

We are looking in the opposite direction from 72955 (pages 52-53) along the Esplanade, with the tower of the town church of Holy Trinity to the left of the clock tower. A few bathing machines survive amongst the beach huts and changing tents.

THE SWIMMING POOL *1938* 88618

Exmouth's sea front swimming pool was built a few years before this photograph was taken, but it has now closed. The white building in the centre of the photograph is the Royal Beacon Hotel, and the hotel on the left, level with the flower beds, is the Channel View.

THE SWIMMING BATHS *c1955* E52024

These swimming baths used sea water, and were designed for international competitions. The pool had a length of just over 50 yards and a width of just 20 yards. An earlier bathing pool was built in Exmouth in 1842, offering hot and cold sea water baths.

ESPLANADE GARDENS *c1950* E52020

It is busy day on Exmouth sea front, a foretaste of how the wider use of motor vehicles was to dominate such seaside towns in the latter half of the 20th century. Apart from the design of the cars, not much has changed on this section of Exmouth sea front.

PAVILION GARDENS
c1955 E52025

Exmouth enjoyed live theatre quite early on, as seaside resorts go. Long before the sea front Pavilion Theatre was built, a small playhouse existed in the Parade in the centre of the town at the very beginning of the 19th century. The great tragedian Edmund Kean performed on stage there during his tour of South Devon.

THE PAVILION *c1955* E52013

The Pavilion was built in 1933 and has recently been renovated. A competition was held for a design for this theatre as early as 1928, with many architects submitting designs. Local councillors frowned at the cost of the winning design, and it was quietly shelved. The town's own surveyor eventually came up with a plan for the present theatre.

ESPLANADE GARDENS *c1965* E52145

The Pavilion remains today an important venue for plays and concerts, surrounded by lovely gardens and with the beach and sea just across the road.

THE HARBOUR VIEW CAFÉ *c1955* E52018

The Harbour View began its existence as a sea water bath emporium, and was latterly the clubhouse for the Exmouth Yacht Club. It has been a café for well over half a century. The notice board tells us that ice creams, coffee and waffles are available. This view of the prominent sea front café is remarkably unchanged - even the old lamps remain on site.

THE MINIATURE RAILWAY *1960* E52099

All of this area of the sea front is now part of the Exmouth Fun Park, a modest theme park for the young and not so young who want a break from the miles of sandy beaches.

THE BOATING LAKE
c1955 E52104

This boating lake has survived as part of the present-day Exmouth Fun Park. Beyond and to the left is the lifeboat station, built in 1903 and still in use for the inshore rescue boat and as a visitor centre for the Royal National Lifeboat Institution.

ESPLANADE GARDENS
c1960 E52101

The people of Exmouth have always taken a great pride in the beauties of the gardens along the sea front; each lawn and flowerbed is carefully tended by the skilled workers of the local council. They are grand for relaxation, sun bathing, or just sitting and watching the world go by.

Frithelstock
TORRINGTON
Lit. Torrington
Langtree
Roborough
Burrington
Kings Nympton
CHULMLEIGH
R. Torridge
E.t Putford
W.t Putford
Bulkworthy
Abbots Bickington
Newton St. Petrock
Peters Marland
Beaford
Ashreigney
Cheldon
Chawley
Sutcombe
Milton Damerell
Shebbear
Merton
Huish
Dolton
Dowland
Wembworthy
Eggesford
Thornbury
Buckland Filleigh
Petrockstow
Meeth
Iddesleigh
Winkley
Nymet Rowland
Coleridge
Bradford
Sheepwash
Monk Oakhampton
Brushford
Pancrassweek
Cookbury
Black Torrington
Highampton
Broadwood Kelly
HATHERLEIGH
Bundley
Bridgerule
HOLSWORTHY
Hollacombe
Honeychurch
Zeal Monachorum
Pyworthy
Exbourne
N.th Tawton
Jacobstowe
Sampford Courtenay
BOW or Nymet Tracey
Bude Canal
Deer R.
Clawton
Beaworthy
Northlew
Broad Nymet
Halwell
Inwardleigh
Carey R.
Ashbury
Taw R.
Spreyton
Tetcott
Kigbear
OAKHAMPTON
From Stratton
Ashwater
S.th Tawton
Luffincott
Germans Week
Belstone
Virginstow
Thistle Brook
Cawston Beacon
N.th Petherwin
Bratton Clovelly
Throwley
Drewsteignton
St. Giles on the Heath
Bridestowe
Werrington
Bradwood Widger
Sourton
Yes Tor
Gidley
Riv.r Attery
Thurshelton
Taw Head
Chagford
Stowford
Gr.t Links
Lewtrenchard
Lifton
Lidford
Dart Head
LAUNCESTON
Coryton
From Bodmin
River Lid
Cleave
Mary Stow
Willsworthy
Cut Hill
Manaton
Kelly
Brentor
Bradstone
DARTMOOR
Dunterton
Milton Abbot
Mary Tavy
Widecombe in the Moor
Lamerton
Peter Tavy
Gr.t Mis Tor
River Tamar
Rippon Tor
Sydenham Damarel
Dart Riv.
Webber Riv.
TAVISTOCK
Prison
Canal
Whitechurch
Sampford Spiney
FOREST
From Callington
Walkhampton
Holne
Caters Beam
ASHBURTON
Ryders Hill
Sheepstor
Buckland Monachorum
Meavy
Erme Head
Buckfastleigh
Beer Alston
Riv. Avon
Dean Prior
Shaugh
Yealm H.d
Beer Ferris
Bickleigh
Dartmoor Road
South Brent
Tamerton
WALES

A SECTION OF A DEVONSHIRE COUNTY MAP
Showing Exmouth and surrounding areas c1850

THE BEACH

THE QUALITY of a traditional seaside holiday comes down in the end to the attractiveness of the beach, and Exmouth has one of the finest stretches of sand in Devon. It owes this good fortune to the nearness of the Exe estuary, which has forced back the pebbles which line the strands of many of the other resorts in the east of the county.

But, as we can see in this selection of photographs, a whole infrastructure was put in place for the benefit of bathers. Bathing machines look odd to us now, brought up as we are in a less restricted society, but they were an absolute essential in Victorian and Edwardian times, when bathing (particularly mixed bathing) in full view was frowned upon. Only the wealthier visitors to Exmouth would have been able to afford them - the poorer members of society, and the less prudish, would have changed and bathed without them, either from the dunes around the Maer or in isolated coves such as Sandy Bay.

What is clear from these views, whether they are Victorian, Edwardian or well into the 20th century (and however inhibiting the style of bathing costume portrayed in them), is that a good time has been had on Exmouth's sands for generations.

THE SANDS *1890* 26261

Exmouth has been a popular resort for over two hundred years. Its miles of long sandy beaches, gently sloping sands, and safe bathing offer all that is needed for a perfect seaside holiday. But there would have been little chance of getting sunburned in Victorian times, thanks to the protection offered by these overgenerous costumes.

THE BEACH *1890* 26263

A few bathers brave the sea from a fairly deserted Exmouth beach in the last full decade of Queen Victoria's reign. Bathing machines, such as the ones seen here, flourished from the end of the 18th century until the early years of the 20th century. A bathing machine would be hired by the more prosperous bather, who would change into a cumbersome bathing costume inside it. Then the bathing machine would be wheeled into the sea so that the swimmer might enter the water scarcely seen by passers by and with modesty intact.

THE BEACH *1898* 42464

The smaller bathing machines seen here are bearing advertising posters for Pears Soap, one of the most popular and widely advertised Victorian retail products. Just within the sea are larger, probably cheaper, and communal bathing machines.

◄ **THE BEACH**
1898 42465

Ice cream - or 'Hokey Pokey' as it was known to the Victorians -has long been a popular fare on Exmouth sea front. It would have been sold in a block on a sheet of paper. Here we see the stall of Capocci & Sons, a well-known Italian ice cream maker resident in Exmouth. Capocci's sales cry was 'Hokey Pokey, penny a lump, that's the stuff to make you jump'.

◄ **THE BEACH** *1898* 42462

Beyond the overdressed Victorian beachgoers are a number of stalls selling ice creams and other refreshments. In the distance, to the right beyond the bathing machines, is the distinctive tower of what is now the Harbour View café, at the date of this photograph the lookout for the Coast Watch patrol.

▼ **THE SANDS** *1906* 53938

Photography was still enough of a novelty in Edwardian England for the Frith photographer to get bathers to pose for him - as we can see in this charming picture of young people paddling on the shoreline. The many dinghies and yachts demonstrate Exmouth's importance as a boating resort.

▶ **THE SANDS** *1922* 72956

In the decades following the First World War, Exmouth reached the heights of its fame as a holiday resort, thanks to the greater mobility offered by railway trains and motor vehicles. There was much to do apart from sea bathing; as well as donkey rides, there were boating, sporting activities, country rambles, concerts and plays. Exmouth had established a reputation of offering alternatives if wet and wild weather ruled out a day on the beach.

◀ **THE SANDS AND THE PLEASURE BOATS** *1925* 78600

The sweep of Lyme Bay and the attractions of the Exe estuary had made Exmouth a favoured resort for those who wanted to take to the water for a small voyage. Here we see a passenger boat setting out for a popular 'trip round the bay'. Fishermen could hire a boat such as the one seen here in the foreground for fishing expeditions for bass, pollock and mackerel.

▲ **THE SANDS** *1925* 78601

Exmouth's sandy beaches might have been made for the traditional 'bucket and spade' holiday. These children are clearly delighting in making sand castles, digging holes in the beach for the sea to fill, or just engaging in a spot of amateur beachcombing.

◄ **THE SANDS** *1925* 78599

A number of beach huts and sales stalls served holidaymakers on Exmouth's sands in the heady days before the Second World War. Here we see a refreshment hut and a kiosk selling film. Many of these huts were washed away in a great storm in the 1930s.

▲ **THE SEA FRONT** *1925* 78597

An Exmouth boatman stands barefoot on the Esplanade seeking customers for the many boat trips on offer. This photograph illustrates how the Victorian sea wall was designed to throw back the waves in a Channel gale.

THE BEACH
c1955 E52012

In this view of the beach opposite the Pavilion Theatre, we see the children's miniature fun fair that enjoyed a brief post-war existence on Exmouth's sands - it included swing boats and a roundabout. Even just over fifty years ago, beachgoers were almost as overdressed as their Victorian and Edwardian forebears.

THE SANDS
c1960 E52109

The wind-break, that phenomenon of the mid 20th century, had clearly caught on in Exmouth by the time this photograph was taken at the beginning of the Swinging Sixties. But apart from such modern innovations and less modest costumes, the scene hasn't really changed very much in the seventy years of these beach photographs.

FROM THE CLIFF *1918* 68707

We are looking over Exmouth from the high ground to the east of the resort, with the sands of the Maer, a glorious open space, in the middle distance. The Maer was once a golf course for the town, but it was allowed to revert back to wilderness in the 1950s. The cliff walk now forms part of the South West Coast Path, the national trail which winds around the West Country peninsula.

THE CLIFFS, ORCOMBE POINT *1906* 53971

Exmouth is fortunate to have a wild stretch of coastline to the east, offering walks and wild scenery. The cliffs at Orcombe and the High Land of Orcombe are now a property of the National Trust, offering excellent views across the resort and the neighbouring coastline of south and east Devon.

ORCOMBE POINT *c1960* E52114

A road was built along the foot of these cliffs in the 1920s, allowing access to what had previously been the domain of fishermen and smugglers. Exmouth's museum boasts the ship's wheel of the 'Tehwija', wrecked on this stretch of coastline in 1907.

AN ORDNANCE SURVEY MAP *showing Exmouth and surrounding areas 1904*

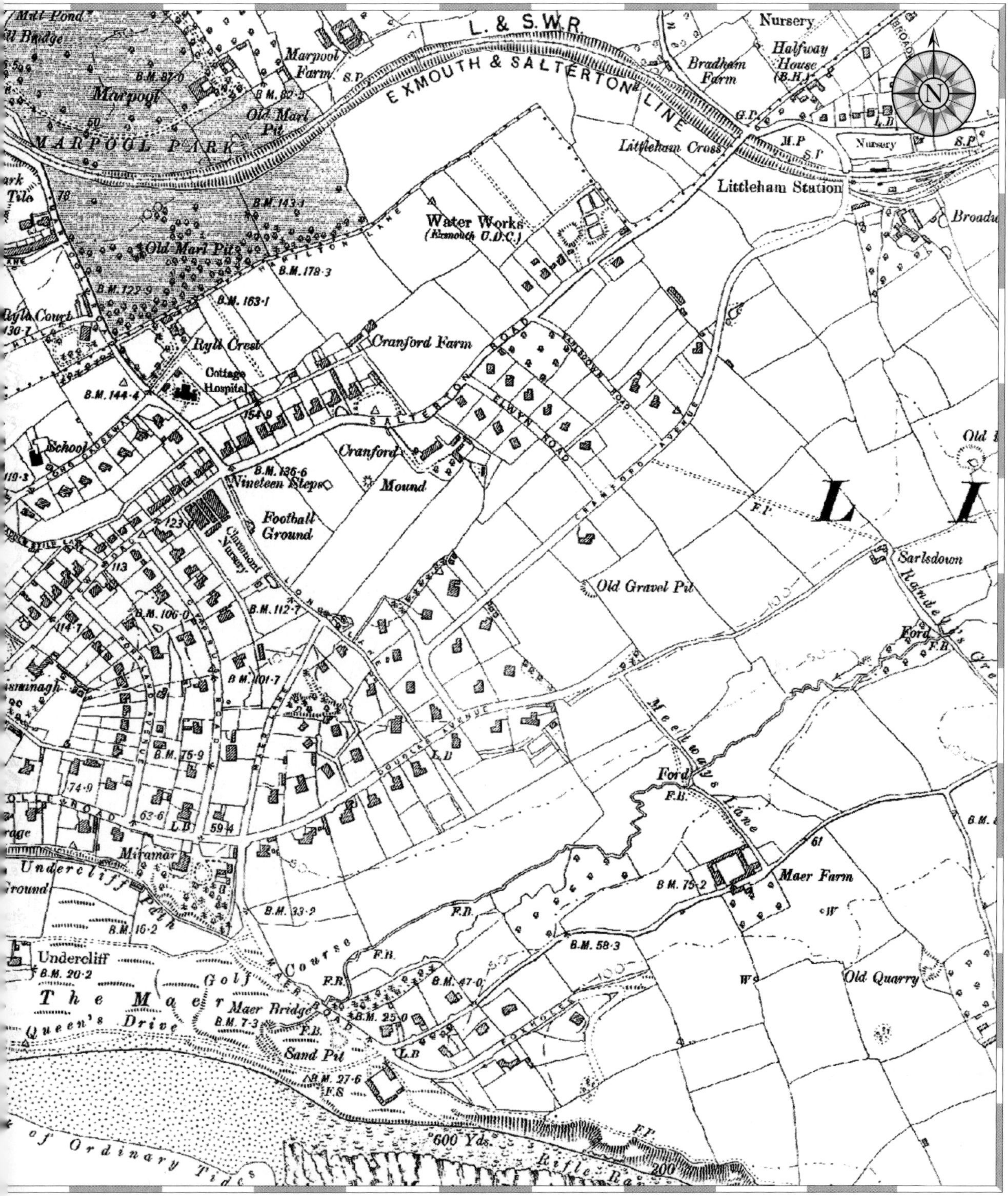
L. & S.W.R.
EXMOUTH & SALTERTON LINE
Marpool
MARPOOL PARK
Marpool Farm
Old Marl Pit
Old Marl Pit
Nursery
Halfway House (B.H.)
Bradham Farm
Littleham Cross
Littleham Station
Nursery
Water Works (Exmouth U.D.C.)
Ryll Court
Ryll Crest
Cottage Hospital
Cranford Farm
School
Cranford
Nineteen Steps
Mound
Football Ground
Old Gravel Pit
Sarlsdown
Ford
Ford
F.B.
Maer Farm
Old Quarry
Miramar
Undercliff
The Maer
Golf Course
Maer Bridge
Queen's Drive
Sand Pit
600 Yds.
Rifle Ra
of Ordinary Tides
L I

LITTLEHAM, *Cottages 1890* 26277

Much of what is now Littleham is relatively modern; however, the original village is much older than Exmouth, and was once much more important. Few of its older buildings remain, though a handful of cottages give a feeling of what ancient Littleham must have looked like.

LITTLEHAM AND ROUND ABOUT

ONE of the great joys of Exmouth is its beautiful setting, caught magnificently between the sea, the long Exe estuary and the wilder countryside of heath and cliff that so defines east Devon, offering wonderful places to explore beyond the confines of the urban seaside resort.

Exmouth began as a suburb of the nearby villages of Littleham and Withycombe Raleigh, though both have now become suburbs of the newer town. Littleham retains its village feel, though only a few ancient cottages have survived to cluster around the even older church. Here is the tomb of Lady Nelson, perhaps the most famous of the many visitors who came to Exmouth and decided to stay. Beyond is Sandy Bay, Littleham's own beach, once a smugglers' cove but now the setting for one of England's largest caravan sites, often echoing with gunfire from the Royal Marines training range on nearby Straight Point.

Wisely, those who planned the growth of suburban Littleham built its modest shopping centre away from the heart of the old village. Between the church and the neighbouring resort of Budleigh Salterton are miles of clifftop walks and lonelier countryside. Long may these areas remain free and undeveloped.

Below the heathlands is the absolutely delightful church of St John in the Wilderness, a haven of peace and tranquillity for all who seek a break from the excitements of the bustling resort of Exmouth; and nearer to the estuary is the strange house of A La Ronde, a trip back in time to those heady days of Georgian elegance and eccentricity.

◄ **LITTLEHAM,** *The Church 1890* 26279

In 1042 Edward the Confessor granted the manor of Littleham to his thane Ordgar. The parish church of Saint Margaret and Saint Andrew dates back to at least 1146, and there may have been an earlier Saxon church on the site. In the graveyard is the tomb of Frances, Lady Nelson, wife of the hero of Trafalgar, who was laid to rest here in 1831.

▼ **LITTLEHAM,** *The Caravan Site, Sandy Bay c1960* L57044

A vast caravanopolis now covers the cliff tops above Sandy Bay, once a smuggling cove and now Littleham's bathing beach. In the distance is Straight Point, a firing range much used by the Royal Marines, who are stationed at nearby Lympstone.

LITTLEHAM
The Cranford Hotel c1965 L57066

The Cranford Hotel on the outskirts of the town began its existence as the Half Way House; it was transformed from a humbler inn to cater for the increase in visitors to the resort and the suburban growth of the town.

LITTLEHAM, *The New Inn c1955* L57013

There were once at least two inns close to Littleham church. The Plough Inn was demolished to allow for the extension of the graveyard, leaving the New Inn a few yards further down towards the sea. Notice the cockerel weathervane - happily still in place half a century onwards.

LITTLEHAM, *The Clinton Arms c1965* L57072

Within a decade, the New Inn had changed its name to the Clinton Arms in honour of the local landowners. This public house has changed very slightly over the years, with a small extension on this side of the building and a glass-fronted veranda facing the car park.

LITTLEHAM
Tythe Cottage c1965
L57069

This charming cottage survives as a local café and teashop, its sweeping thatch still providing shade on hot summer days. It is a reminder of old Littleham and the village that was here before the district became a suburb of Exmouth.

LITTLEHAM, *Littleham Road c1965* L57068

The modern shops of Littleham are some distance away from the heart of the older village. We see here Cranford Parade, not changed much since this photograph was taken, though the shops have new proprietors. On the corner, behind the now vanished telephone box, are the premises of A & W Riches & Son, an ironmonger's, and further down is the shop of V Carter & Sons. Lloyds Bank (centre right) is now Littleham Post Office, and E Prior the newsagent's (right) is now a tropical fish shop.

LITTLEHAM, *The Cliff Path c1955* L57038

Once the cliff paths around Littleham were used by coastguards, who were on constant watch for smuggling activities. Now the paths are part of the South West Coastal Footpath, and lead to Exmouth in one direction and the neighbouring resort of Budleigh Salterton in the other.

A LA RONDE *1906* 53960

This sixteen-sided house was built by the Misses Jane and Mary Parminter in the 1790s. The rooms surround an octagonal central hall over sixty feet high, which is topped by a shell-covered gallery. Nearby is a chapel, built by the ladies so that they might avoid having to travel into Exmouth for worship - the two eccentric and reclusive women were buried there within a few yards of their strange home.

INDEX

LITTLEHAM AND ROUND ABOUT

NAMES OF SUBSCRIBERS

The following people have kindly supported this book by subscribing to copies before publication:

Mr and Mrs D Adams, Exmouth
Alan and Rebecca
Cyril J Anderson
Lillian Anderson, from your loving Family
Charles and Elizabeth Aylesbury
David S Baker, Exmouth
The Bamsey Family, Exmouth
Peter Bateman
Mr and Mrs G E Bennett, Exmouth
Berridge's 2006
The Betts Family, Exmouth
Mr and Mrs Bolt and Family, Exmouth
James Bradford, Exmouth
Ross Brown, Little Angel, Always with us
Gill and Trevor Brown
Tina Burke, Exmouth
Brian E Cain
Stephen F Cain
Don and Wendy Capper
In memory of Bessie and Russel Carter
Peter Casely
Michael Chanter
Mike and Jackie Chapman, Exmouth
Michael and Valerie Clarke, née King, Exmouth
All the best, Claire and Russell Clarke
Clinton Guest House, 41 Morton Road, Exmouth
Mr and Mrs J A Coad, Exmouth
Tom Cobley, Cranford Cottage, Salterton Road
Hugh Davies, Exmouth
Sue and Roy Davis - For Anna, Joel and Chay
John R Decarlo, Washingtonville, NY, USA
Mr C C Deem, Littleham, Exmouth
Oodles of love, Dibsy xx
The Doran Family, Exmouth
To Norman Drew, 80 years young!
Mrs Frances Fellows
Janice and Jim Ferris, Exmouth
Mr C D and Mrs M E Finch, Exmouth
Mr John V Fletcher
Dr Ian Foster
Exmouth Town Crier, F Tregarthen Gibson
Love to Toby James Gowers, Born 13/11/05, love from Mum and Dad
To Bernadette Grumbt, Happy 40th birthday, love from Dave, Natasha and Adam
Roy and Jackie Heaton
Happy Birthday Tim Helliwell, from mother Joan
Marjorie Holman
The Hughes Family, our best move in 1997
Eric John Crosby James
Conrad and Nicola Jones, Exmouth
Ruth M Kelly
In Memory of Reg King
The Kirk Family, Exmouth
Denis Lander, Exmouth
Wing Cdr and Mrs D Laskey, Remember N & D Abbott
David Chown Lee, Exmouth
Mr John Arthur Ley
To Lee, lots of love, Victoria and Libby
In memory of Lily and Win - our Mothers
In Memory of my Father, Norman R London
Dick Manning, love Paul, Julie, Shannon and Jack
P S McMillan, Exmouth, For summers long ago.
Robert and Joy Moass, Exmouth
Richard and Alison Moss
A tribute to my wife Elizabeth Nelson
Jenny Newman
Jennifer Norton, Exmouth
The Family of Ian Oglivie born Exmouth 1921
David and Joan Owen, "Charters", Exmouth
D T M Packer, Builders, Exmouth
The Parkinson Family, Exmouth
Marian and Hywel Parry-Jones, January 2006
To Pat, happy birthday, love Carole
Geoff Perriman
Joan Blumire, to Doris and Sydney Philips
Anita Rainbow
To Darren Reed, with love from Abi
In memory of Vicki Rendall, Exmouth
Mr and Mrs Tony Rich and Family
Dennis Rich and Family
Marlene Richards, Exmouth, Devon
Alan Richardson
Brian Leonard Rowsell
Helen Rushton, Exmouth, On her birthday
Christine Sedgemore
Barry and Margaret Setter, née Thorn
Shirley Peter, Sam, Lee and Dusty
Christine Simpson
Mrs Doreen A Slade, Mel, Brad and Cassandra
Rosemary and Bryan Snow
Maurice Southwell, Withycombe Raleigh
Jeanne Stanbury
In memory of Cllr, Prof P J Stoy 1906 - 2000
Robert Stuart
The Thorn Family, Exmouth
Mary Eileen Joan Vaughan
In memory of Eric and Lucy Watkins
Christine M Weller, Exmouth
Kevin West, Exmouth
To Martin West on his 60th birthday
Jan and Martin White
Michael Derek Williams
Anne Wilmot and Family, Exmouth
Elly Wilmott
To Win
Chris Wright, Exmouth Funpark, The Seafront

FREE PRINT OF YOUR CHOICE

Mounted Print
Overall size 14 x 11 inches (355 x 280mm)

Choose any Frith photograph in this book. Simply complete the Voucher opposite and return it with your remittance for £2.25 (to cover postage and handling) and we will print the photograph of your choice in SEPIA (size 11 x 8 inches) and supply it in a cream mount with a burgundy rule line (overall size 14 x 11 inches). **Please note: photographs with a reference number starting with a "Z" are not Frith photographs and cannot be supplied under this offer.**
Offer valid for delivery to one UK address only.

***PLUS:* Order additional Mounted Prints at HALF PRICE - £7.49 each** (normally £14.99)
If you would like to order more Frith prints from this book, possibly as gifts for friends and family, you can buy them at half price (with no additional postage and handling costs).

***PLUS:* Have your Mounted Prints framed**
For an extra £14.95 per print you can have your mounted print(s) framed in an elegant polished wood and gilt moulding, overall size 16 x 13 inches (no additional postage and handling required).

IMPORTANT!

These special prices are only available if you use this form to order. You must use the ORIGINAL VOUCHER on this page (no copies permitted). We can only despatch to one UK address. This offer cannot be combined with any other offer.

Send completed Voucher form to:
The Francis Frith Collection, Frith's Barn, Teffont, Salisbury, Wiltshire SP3 5QP

CHOOSE A PHOTOGRAPH FROM THIS BOOK

Voucher *for **FREE** and Reduced Price Frith Prints*

Please do not photocopy this voucher. Only the original is valid, so please fill it in, cut it out and return it to us with your order.

Picture ref no	Page no	Qty	Mounted @ £7.49	Framed + £14.95	Total Cost £
		1	Free of charge*	£	£
			£7.49	£	£
			£7.49	£	£
			£7.49	£	£
			£7.49	£	£
			£7.49	£	£
			* Post & handling		£2.25
			Total Order Cost		£

Please allow 28 days for delivery. Offer available to one UK address only

Title of this book ....
I enclose a cheque/postal order for £ ....
made payable to 'The Francis Frith Collection'

OR please debit my Mastercard / Visa / Maestro card, details below

Card Number

Issue No (Maestro only) Valid from (Maestro)

Expires Signature

Name Mr/Mrs/Ms ....
Address ....
....
....
.... Postcode ....
Daytime Tel No ....
Email ....

ISBN 1-84589-035-3 Valid to 31/12/08

Free Print - see overleaf

Can you help us with information about any of the Frith photographs in this book?

We are gradually compiling an historical record for each of the photographs in the Frith archive. It is always fascinating to find out the names of the people shown in the pictures, as well as insights into the shops, buildings and other features depicted.

If you recognize anyone in the photographs in this book, or if you have information not already included in the author's caption, do let us know. We would love to hear from you, and will try to publish it in future books or articles.

Our production team

Frith books are produced by a small dedicated team at offices in the converted Grade II listed 18th-century barn at Teffont near Salisbury, illustrated above. Most have worked with The Francis Frith Collection for many years. All have in common one quality: they have a passion for The Francis Frith Collection. The team is constantly expanding, but currently includes:

Andrew Alsop, Paul Baron, Jason Buck, John Buck, Heather Crisp, David Davies, Natalie Davis, Louis du Mont, Isobel Hall, Chris Hardwick, Lucy Hart, Julian Hight, Peter Horne, James Kinnear, Karen Kinnear, Tina Leary, Stuart Login, Sue Molloy, Sarah Roberts, Kate Rotondetto, Dean Scource, Eliza Sackett, Terence Sackett, Sandra Sampson, Adrian Sanders, Sandra Sanger, Julia Skinner, Lewis Taylor, Shelley Tolcher, Lorraine Tuck, Miranda Tunnicliffe, Will Tunnicliffe, David Turner and Ricky Williams.